Only You Girl

Only You Girl

BJ

To order additional copies of this book, contact:
Xlibris Corporation
1-888-795-4274
www.Xlibris.com
Orders@Xlibris.com
37684

Contents

Dedicating this book:

To all the people in my life,
Some having part in these
Stories . . . you are all loved!

Thanks to you all for the good times.

BJ

I wondered where to start this story; there's only one place, from my heart. As I've gone through life, it seemed to me that at least once in a while I would do something right! Oh sure I have, but as I look back now, I realize that the fun times were when someone was giving me____! (You fill in the blank—something usually found underneath horses.) My family says I draw the stuff from people, something to do with the look on my face. I can't see it, but more than one has said so. My girlfriend Terry always says, "Only you girl." The reason being that no one could walk through life and have so many such silly things happen to her.

Only You Stories

"Only you" stories start. We were having a "Pampered Chef" party at my girlfriend's house, and Terry started to bring up a story. Of course, the party host was trying to give her presentation, and we were all telling stories—you see the picture. Terry said that I should tell this particular story, as she couldn't tell it as good as I. It didn't take me long to help out. I told the girls about the time Terry and I were talking about how I couldn't get back to sleep once I have woke up, and she told me that whenever she gets up in the night to go to the bathroom, she doesn't let her self wake up. Well, I have to get up at least two times a night to go. So I asked her, "How do you keep from waking up?" She said she doesn't turn on any lights and doesn't think about anything, if she could help it. Anyway, a couple of nights after that, I got up to go, and I started to think about what Terry said. So I went in the bathroom without turning on the light. (Now when I have to go, I have to go!) Thinking not to think, I sat down and relieved myself. I jumped up and now I was awake because there was some warm stuff everywhere—down my legs, all over the toilet, on the floor, and my bare feet are getting sticky! I said, "Who put the lid down?" Nobody in my house ever puts the lid down! And of course now I was wide-awake! The lady giving the party and every guest was laughing. OK, we were trying to have a demo here please. Then one of the girls said, "Now I know the real girl."

The Doctors Visit

Like the time I had to have repeat appointments at the doctor's for an existing problem (won't mention reason). Well anyway, I was having my test, and the doctor said she would be back after I got dressed to do some blood work. So I got dressed and then had to go to the bathroom, which I did. A few days later, I phoned up the clinic and asked for my blood work results; the nurse left the phone to get my records. Then she came back on the phone and said, "We can't find them, are you sure you came in?" Yes and OK, she would look again. Finally, she came back on the phone and said, "Girl, are you sure you had the tests drawn?" Ding went the bell, as I remembered that I had left the bathroom that day, and no, I hadn't had the blood work done! Talk about which shade of red! The next time I had an appointment, the doctor opened the door and peeked her head around and said, "You left!" I was sort of laughing, and after this checkup, same thing. "We will be back to do some blood work," she said (she and the nurse) with a certain look on her face. So OK, I'd stay but first I needed to go to the bathroom. When I opened the bathroom door, the doctor and the nurse were standing right in front of it! You aren't getting away again! Have you ever!

Riding the Bike

On about my fifty-fifth birthday, I told my husband Shane that I wanted a ten-speed for the special occasion. We went to Wally World to pick out this bike. I pulled one out of the rack and started trying it out in the aisle to make sure I have the right size. Shane saw this and walked the other way, as stuff like this embarrassed him. "Yep, this is the one, we'll take it." We were about home, and I told Shane to stop so I could ride the bike the rest of the way. Shane said, "Are you sure?" And of course I am. We unloaded the bike, and I got on and started to ride. Shane started down the road; we had about three-fourths of a mile to go. My knees kept coming up and hitting the handlebars, and it hurt! I couldn't seem to figure out how to ride without this happening (couldn't straighten legs, knees bumping handlebars). I was calling out, "SHANE, COME BACK!" Of course he couldn't hear me and paid no attention if I was making it or not! It's downhill to our driveway, so I made that all right but the climb up the long drive. By the time I walked my new bike up the drive and got into our shop, I was plenty tuckered out. I said to Shane, "My knees kept hitting the handlebars, and I tried the bike in the store, what the hell is wrong?" Shane's not paying any attention, so I went upstairs. The next day, we were back in the shop, and my new bike was standing up against the wall, so I went over and looked at it, and I saw numbers on the handlebars that looked different than they did the day before. So I was telling him that I could have sworn that yesterday those numbers were on the other side and these were on this side. And also the curved hand bars were facing up instead of down! By now, I had his attention; he came over and took the handlebars and swung them around! He said, "Did you ride the bike with the front wheel backward?" Now the numbers were on the other side again! Of course everybody had a great time giving me—over that one too!

Safeway's

See, I have this thing about not being able to keep my mouth shut. I have to tell all, like the time I went into Safeway's store to shop. They had these new shopping carts. I pulled one out and tried to get the top down and couldn't, so I guess these things don't hold so much stuff in the top compartment. I went walking around the store and here came the manager, and I said to him, "I hate your new carts!" He reached over and grabbed the top and dropped it down! You go girl. I don't think that I will ever live that one down. It's my daughter Jen's favorite story.

Neighborhood

When I was growing up in the neighborhood, there was a bunch of girls and several boys; we were quite the crew, always playing some sort of ball and building forts and huts, sleigh riding, whatever. We had what we girls called "our Jell-O tree." We always got Jell-O packages from our mom's cupboards, and off to the tree we'd go. There we would spend countless hours licking Jell-O out of our hands and talking and laughing about the boys, etc. I would still like to see the farmer's face when he started harvesting his apples, and every year there was a pile of empty Jell-O boxes under this one certain tree! Go figure!

You know I could babysit just about any night of the week, being there were a lot of young parents in the neighborhood. We made a quarter an hour back then, some odd fifty years ago. My dad told me that if I would start a savings account with my babysitting money, I would have money for beauty school. He said he would match whatever I saved. Well, at a quarter an hour, it took awhile to save sixty dollars, but I did. And then whenever Maggie and I wanted candy for the school assembly or movie, we would go to the savings account and get a dollar or so. Anyway, one day Dad wanted to know how much I had saved, I told him, "None now." He really thought I was telling a fib when I said, "I spent it on candy." I candied up to 140 pounds. I did go to beauty school, though, sixteen years later. I believe I probably had one of the finest childhood a person could have.

My first crush, Darrell. He gave me my first kiss. Walking home from a church gathering, there were several of us, and he kissed me on the lips, have you. I slapped his face, and he slapped mine back! I just got the obituary from Mom in the mail; he just passed away with cancer. I'm so glad that he was part of my life. He used to torture me to death when the snow came, wash my face and throw snowballs at me until I was scared to even get off the bus from school. I would trade clothes with the kids so maybe he wouldn't recognize me. That didn't work, so finally Dad and Mom had to call his parents for a conference. The snowballs stopped.

Halloween

The neighborhood girls decided to have a Halloween party. Dad and Mom said we could use the garage for the party. We planned and rearranged the garage, did the shopping, and invited everyone in the neighborhood. We were to have root beer floats along with the other goodies. We bought the big eighteen-ounce bottles. Put the ice cream and root beer in the freezer. Our floats didn't go over very well as when we opened the freezer to get the stuff, the freezer was nothing but a root beer sud. The bottles had burst, and what a mess we had left to clean up. The party was fun though.

Christmastime

Our folks always did the holidays up real good for us kids. My sis, Barbara, would get so excited that she would be shaking the morning of. I would always be asking to get up early, starting about 1:00 am. Usually around 3:00 a.m., we would get to get up. We had to wait for each other so no one was left out.

Every year I would spend much of the time getting ready for Christmas by sneaking in everything I could think of to find the presents. Barbara would tell me that it wasn't nice to sneak at Christmas. I really couldn't help myself. (I can hear my sis as she reads this. Going, oh sure. You couldn't help it.) I figured out one year that all our stuff was hidden in Dad and Mom's little camping trailer. Come Christmas morning though, there wasn't anything of our presents that's the same. They had put our kids' stuff in Uncle Jim's trailer, and they had put theirs in Dad's and Mom's! Tricked me. The last year that I was home for the holiday was the best though! I had asked for a cedar chest the year before, but didn't get it. This year, I wasn't even thinking of the chest. I had looked at every present under the tree before Christmas had even come. These were the gifts given to us by friends, brothers and sisters, whoever. Not Santa Claus! So come that special morning. I was opening my gifts, and I noticed that I already knew what every one of them were! Everyone else was still opening theirs. I tried not to show it, but I was thinking that because there weren't any more for me, that I had finally got what I deserved. No more presents (for peeking). Then Dad said to me, "I think maybe there is something in the tree. Maybe that's yours." I got up and looked. There was an envelope with my name on it. I opened this, and there was a key inside with the word "Lane" printed on it. There's a note that said, "If you can find it, this key belongs to it, and it's yours." Now I really got to look for presents. I went all over the house. Finally in the garage under a blanket was my cedar chest! My dad had won a baseball board, and that's how they got it for me. Isn't that the greatest story?

One year at Christmastime, I decided to give Shane some hot rollers for the occasion. This was a payback for the year before when he had tricked me. Along about July, I had noticed a $29.95 withdrawal in our checkbook. I asked him what this was for. His answer was none of my business! This was a mystery and not the usual. So I figured that he was up to a surprise. On Christmas morning, I got a spray gun from him! The first thing I said was, "this was the none of my business charge!" He figured he made up for it by giving me a .22-250 rifle also!

My little brothers, Ed and Jeff, were always getting into Mom's goodie pantry. She would go to make a batch of cookies or candy, cake, etc. Many of these times, the chocolate chips would be all gone. She finally had a lock put on the door. They then took off the hinges to get their treats. So one day, she decided to really hide this batch of fudge, being she had to have it for her club gathering. Mom decided to hide the fudge in the dryer. After all, she's the only one who used the dryer. My other sister Linda decided to come home for the day and do her wash. Mom had gone to town for some shopping. When she came home and opened the front door and heard the dryer going, you can almost see the look on her face. She had the biggest fudge mess in the whole world!

Horses

I could say that horses have played a big part in my life, starting with the day when my friend Linda came to my house and asked me if I wanted to go riding with her. I said sure, but I had never been on a horse. My first question was, how do I get on it? We looked around and I decided to go get the ladder. Our road was paved, and with all the houses around, I felt a little foolish, but I set up the ladder and climb up and on behind Maggie. We were on our way, I looked back and there the ladder still stood in the street! We went for miles enjoying ourselves. Along came a guy in a neat car, and as he went by, we yelled, "Get a horse!" The guy (a teenager) turned around and pulled alongside us. He jumped out and took the reins, mounted and said, "Have fun!" We were so excited by this attention that we got in his car and drove all over the town. We started to think about him and the horse, so we headed back toward home and found the rider and horse. He thanked us, laughing the whole time. We never did ask him his name!

After my husband Shane and I got married, his brother Dahl sold us a mare named Dancer. I got her out one day and took off riding her. Well, there was a freeway about a block up the road from us. Shane was lying on the lawn, and as I got near the underpass of the freeway, a big rig went overhead and a small red car came underneath the overpass. Well, Dancer, the horse, freaked out and took off up the hill to the freeway. Note: a short way up! I had but one choice, and that's to get off! I took a leap sideways and hung on to her reins, keeping her from death (not to count me). I got the horse home, and there's Shane lying on the lawn, with his head propped by his hand, watching all of this. I said to him, "Couldn't you have helped me?" "What was I supposed to do?" he said. Then one day I overheard him talking about the overpass, seemed there were some rattlesnakes under it! You can guess where the rest of the story went. Anyway on to another Dancer story. Have you ever planted a garden, only to wake up the morning the corn is to be harvested, to find the horse eating the whole roll of corn! She didn't get any hay fed that day. Another time, Shane decided to come and get me on the horse. We lived in North Idaho by then and had bought some acreage. We had a driveway of about 1,600 feet. It took a long time to get this driveway so that you could use it in the spring. This time of the year was called spring breakup (when the frost is coming out of the ground.) Mud season is more what I call it! We had to park the rigs on the county road and walk to the place. I was late getting home from work, it's raining, and I had two armloads of groceries to pack in. I was given this nice long coat, and I had just had it dry-cleaned. Wearing this coat, I was trekking my way through the mud and snow in the dark. My arms were getting tired, and I came over this little hill (as I had taken a short cut), and there was Shane on our horse, standing there in the rain. I was so surprised! I thanked him for coming to help me. He said to hand him the grocery bags, and about the time I stepped closer to do just that, I slipped and down the hill I went. Clean new coat was now totally mud covered all over the back. Well, he tried.

We had a lot of adventures with our horses, but none as scary as the day we decided to meet our friends Chuck and Pat up to the lake for breakfast. They drove their motor home, and we rode our horses. We had to cross the highway to get there. It's a busy truck thruway. We did OK crossing and got to the lake. Shane's halfway tied the horses up to some bush twigs, thinking they won't go anywhere. We had two new horses we were training, and Shane had one tied to the other, just so it could come along. Plus I rode our horse Misty. The guys took off fishing after breakfast, and not long we heard some hoof beats. I took a look, and the two, tied together, were heading down the mountain! I yelled to the guys and took off on a slight run to maybe catch them. Here came Shane on my Misty, going after them. The rest of us waited at camp, it seemed forever. Finally we packed the stuff up and headed down the hill. When we got home, there was Shane, the horses, and the story. He was not far behind them, but couldn't catch them. He was worrying about what was going to happen when they reached the highway. He could hear the traffic and just knew there was going to be a terrible accident. Then he heard the high-pitched squeals and screams. Then he was on them. Being that they had been tied together, they got to the hill, just above the highway, and there was a telephone pole, one went on one side and the other took the other side. When they hit each other wrapped around the pole, they must have had a terrific headache, but thanks, no one got killed. We still have horses, and I am now starting out with a very old horse. Wish me luck. OK, I better tell this one: We decided to downsize on the horses, so I made a Horses for Sale sign, putting our phone number at the bottom. We hung it on the fence. A few days later, our daughter Jenny was coming up the stairs, laughing and talking about the sign. "Mom, do you know what that Horses for Sale sign says? It says, 'Hores for Sale.' Phone number was not the right number either. She and her family just giving me what for!" I said it does not! "You spelled 'horses' 'hores,'" she said. I told them, "Oh, I left out the other s!" Jenny picked up the phone and started calling someone. I asked, "Who are you calling?" She's calling the number to see who got the' Hores for Sale' calls! The next day, my friend Etta Mae and I went golfing; she stood up in our women's club, and announced that she had a story to tell. I guess you know which story! I probably won't ever forgive her for that one. But come to think of it, I have a great one on her. We had finished golfing this one day, and I was in the clubhouse waiting for Etta Mae to come in so we could have lunch. Her purse was sitting there on the table, and I kept looking around to see what was taking her so long. She walked in, and laughing she said, "She has been running around with me too long!" As she went down to the cart shed to put away her golf cart and when she got the shed door opened, she turned around and no cart! She had to walk back up the hill and get her cart; she had walked down the hill to put it away! I said, "That outdoes anything I have ever done."

Well, except the day we were walking down the fairway and it started to sprinkle. I pulled out my umbrella and opened it up. Like from the sky came tampons falling all around me! I looked up on the green above me to see if anyone was looking, and hurriedly picked them up! I still don't know how they got in my umbrella!

Tricksters

We girls used to go to one another's house for coffee each and every morning. At Christmastime one year, my friend Linda and her husband Bob came up in the evening for coffee. The guys decided to go to the woodshop to make a rocking duck for the kids. Linda and I sat upstairs talking and decided to build a helper for the guys. We got a jacket and some gloves, a Styrofoam head, put a hair wig on it, then we painted a face on it. We named her Shirley. She was a smoker, so we put a cigarette between her fingers. With the jacket on and sitting at the table, she looked pretty good. We were waiting for the guys to come back upstairs and see their new helper. They're taking a long time to finish evidently, so we decided to sneak down the stairs and listen to what guys talk about when we weren't there. We sat on the stairs looking at each other for forty-five minutes! Finally my husband said, "Women, who can understand them?" Linda's husband said, "Who'd even try?" That was it, not another word out of their mouths. Can you believe it! They did enjoy Shirley though.

At Halloween time, my girlfriend Ginger and I were completely bored due to constantly tricking our friends throughout the year. I wonder now how any of them put up with us. There were four of us girls who hung out together. Living only a few blocks of each other, we would always be together. We got the idea one evening to go for a walk around the neighborhood, as we knew that Verla's (another sidekick) girls were sleeping out on the lawn. We dressed up as men. We put on men's suit, jackets, nylon stocking over our heads, men's hats and proceeded to go scare the girls. My husband had a phony hand, the kind that looks real. We took this with us, and as we were walking along the sidewalk, ready to pass the girls, we heard them saying to each other, "Who's that coming?" About that time I gave the hand a sideway sling, the hand landed right on top of the sleeping bags. The girls started screaming, and they jumped out of the bags and went running into the house. We could hear them yelling "Mom, Mom," scared to death! Then we heard Verla saying, "Settle down, it's just Ginger and Boo." Then we decided to go on down a couple of blocks to Linda's. We knocked on her door, and as she answered it, we acted like we were rushing in. Remember we had on nylon stockings over our heads. After we frightened her, we started laughing, and she chewed us out some. This was always done in fun. Then one evening, our husbands were at work; they were all gone on jobs, as some worked afternoon shifts at the steel plant. Ginger and I went to Linda's for coffee. We visited awhile and then left for home only to turn the car around at the first corner, park, and run to the backside of Linda's house and scratch on the screen. We knew that she wouldn't think it was us. She got so scared that she was dialing the phone for the law, and her hand was shaking so hard she couldn't even dial! So we let her know that it was us and decided we had pushed this fun too far. Besides, she was calling us some pretty good names. They always called me Boo! To this day, that is still my name with the girls.

We used to take the kids and go to the drive-end movie. We phoned Bob and Linda one evening, asking if they would like to go to the movie. Linda said that she did, but Bob wouldn't because he had the "runs." Well, anytime he didn't want to do something, he had another case of them. Linda was always annoyed by this action of his. Anyway one other evening, I called her and asked if she wants to go to the movie. She hesitated some, but yes, she would go with us. At the movie, Linda kept going inside to the snack bar. I started to wonder what the heck she was doing. So the next time she went in, I went after her. Sure enough, into the bathroom booth she went. I went into the one next to her and stood up on the toilet and looked over to see (for fun as usual). There she was with her butt in the air, she's leaning down looking under the booth to see where the feet went next door. About this same time, I started laughing at this site of my friend. Linda threatened to kill me, and I wouldn't blame her if she did. The moral of the story is, Linda said the reason she kept going to the bathroom is: she had the runs and wasn't about to say so because we would give her a bad time (kind of like Bob!). He was so bad that he insisted that he didn't have any crutches of any kind! To let you know to what extremes he would carry this, he used to work in construction. It's lunchtime; Bob's having his lunch in his big dump truck and up popped a female worker on the step with her sack lunch. She opened the door, proceeding to join him, and he told her to take a hike! He shared this story with Linda, and she said to him that was rude! His reply was he wasn't having the guys thinking nil of him. Linda was always talking about how he wouldn't even take an aspirin when he had a headache! So one day, she slipped him a diet pill in his lunch, just to get even. A bunch of us had gathered at their house on a Sunday morning for coffee. Her brother Jim and his wife Sue were there, all of us from the neighborhood. We were talking and laughing about all the good times we had. I decided to tell Bob about the time several years ago that Linda had slipped him a diet pill (thinking he could take a joke). While I was telling this story, someone kicked me under the table. I knew it was Linda but too late! Bob had a discussed look on his face and said,

"Well, it didn't do her any good, did it?" I was laughing and said, "Well, Linda said that you didn't take a nap that day and you even hung a lamp!" You can guess, yes, he left the room mad as hell, Linda having a heart attack fit at me for telling. But as the years went by, we enjoyed this story on Bob immensely!

We girls did the craziest things, Linda and I used to have bread-making contests (this was by hand). You had to make batch after batch and continue baking all day. The last time for me, I had baked thirty loaves and called her up to beat her record. "Guess what, Linda? I just made thirty loaves." Not quite, as thirty-one was her amount! Forget it that was too much for me. We would then put the bread in our freezer. Neither one of us had to bake for a while! One morning I went to her house, and she was covered in flour and exasperated, I could tell. I asked her what the mess was. There was brown paper bag on the floor underneath her breadboard half-full of pie dough. She was still trying to roll out dough! I told her I would make the pies, and she said she'd do my cookies. I always burned my last batch of cookies!

Another time we were having coffee again, and she had a headache, so she got up and got in the cupboard to get a couple of aspirins. She asked me if I wanted a couple too. I looked at her as if "huh," and she said she had an aunt and every time Linda took any medicine, her aunt would say, "That sounds good, give me a couple!"

Speaking of medicine, it reminds me of Linda. She was the most crazy, fun, beautiful person in the world. She was so accident-prone that one time, she was walking through the dining room with a toothpick in her mouth. It dropped out and she stepped on it, straight in her foot. Another time, she was canning and trying to pop a lid off a bottle using a fork. The fork slipped, and she stabbed herself in the chest with it! Another time, a friend told her she should apply for the job at the powder plant. The friend got her an application paper, and as a joke, Linda filled out the paper with all sorts of funnies.

Name: Marilyn
Hair: Blonde
Height: 5'2"

Why did she want to work for this company? So she can have lunch breaks, etc. Well anyway, the friend saw the application and took it to work with her, gave it to her boss for fun. The boss said that anyone with that kind of sense of humor, he wanted to meet! He hired her. She worked for the plant about six months and stepped up on a bucket to reach an item, fell off the thing, and broke her ankle! That's the beginning of several operations, one thing led to another. She ended up getting breast cancer in both breasts and had to have a total mastectomy. They told her maybe in six months she could have reconstructive surgery, and she wasn't having any of it. Years later, she called me up one day and said "Guess what?" I said, "You have boobs!" (Right off the top of my head.) Yes, yes, she did. I was so happy for her. The next time I talked to her, she had to have another surgery to remove them. The gel had leaked and she was itching all over. A few years later, her grandson had a friend over to their house, and as the boys were going through the laundry room, the little friend said to the grandson, "Your grandma doesn't have any boobs." And he said back to him, "Yes, she does. They are right here." He grabbed Linda's special filled bra off the dryer, holding it up and said, "Here they are, right here!" We had a lot of good laughs over that one.

Another time, Linda's husband Bob pulled one on me. I was in their bathroom, which is situated next to the kitchen. I came out of the bathroom only to find him standing on a stepstool, looking in a vent, which looked like he could see in the bathroom at me. I was mortified, I fell lock, stock and barrel as they said, "He couldn't really see into the bathroom."

Speaking of trickster stuff, I'm always trying to get one on by husband Shane. He was always spraying me with the hose or pouring water over the shower, etc. On a nice hot afternoon, he was in the front yard and I was around back. I spotted the garden hose, and thought about getting even. My little girl, Jenny, was about old enough to talk some, so I told her to go tell Daddy that Mama was hurt! She's running around to the front of the house, and I'd turned on the hose. I lay down on the lawn with the hose beside me. Here came Shane with a real concerned look, and as he got to me, I sprayed him good! The look on his face was priceless. For paybacks, one day I was taking a shower. I started to hear some little noises. I looked out of the curtain, and there was Jenny crawling through a laundry shoot. I could barely hear her dad whispering to her to close the drawers. (I had pulled them open in front of the door so no one could get in.) I whispered to Jen, "No, sis," and Shane's fun was spoiled. OK, I have finally learned not to cry "WOLF," learning this the hard way. One afternoon I had been upstairs cleaning, and as I was fixing to go downstairs, I scooped up both my daughters, Jenny and Angie. One in each arm and headed down the stairs, I missed the first step and proceeded to fall on my back all the way down. I was holding the girls up in my arms so they won't take the bunt of the fall! I couldn't move my neck! We had four young sons playing in the basement. They heard the thump, thump from my fall and came running up to see what was going on. It's like in a bad movie. I was lying there, by now letting go of the girls, and all the kids' faces were totally close, surrounding me. I told them to call their dad at his shop. I was still lying there for the longest time. I finally heard Shane come in the kitchen door. Finally some help to get up. The next thing I heard was Shane asking his partner Jack if he wanted some coffee. I hollered at him to help me, nothing—. He thought I was pulling another stunt!

While the guys were at work every day, us girls got together to have coffee. This was a special time to me. One morning, I had finished all my household chores, and it was coffee time, so I got out to the car, jumped in, and started the car out the driveway. I heard a clunk sound under the hood. Didn't think much of it and pulled into Linda's driveway. I heard the sound again. While we were having our "busy bee hour," I mentioned the sound to Linda's husband Bob. He said he would check. I said, "Oh no, it's fine." So I headed home. There lying in our driveway were these funny-looking cables, stretched out from the garage! Oh, that's what the clunk was, battery cables. Shane had hooked up to the battery charger. I really didn't want him to know about this. But the time he really got mad at me was when our friends Kathy and Blaine came over. Blaine and Shane were in the driveway, fixing on Blaine's pickup. We girls decided to go to the Dairy Queen for French fries. Kathy asked me what rig we would take. I said, "Oh, we can take the Buick." Out to the car we went, I started it up and proceeded to back out. The car stopped going; I opened the door, looked back to see if maybe I had a flat tire. Nothing's unusual on my side. "Kathy, is there a flat on your side?" "Nope." So I tried to go again. Still nothing, all of a sudden, I remembered that Shane told me not to take the Buick because he had taken the radiator out to work on it. I lay my head down in Kathy's lap, laughing hysterically! She's going "what is going on?" I said, "Hurry, get out of the car, and let's get in the house 'cause Shane is going to kill me!" As we were going in, our son Pete noticed the deal and went running around back where the guys were at this time, yelling to his dad, "Mom just drove the Buick!" Here came Shane, hollering all kinds of things about me being told not to take the car. And now all the oil was on the ground! When I got kind of nervous about something like that, sometimes I would go into hysterical laughter, probably to keep from crying. This was one of those times. One day a few weeks later, I got ready to go to town, and I stopped by the garage to tell Shane where I was going. He said to me, "See this." I looked at the workbench where he was working on the dash of his pickup. He had the whole dash out and sitting there. Well, what did he mean by that? To which I said, "Yea, I see that, and so, what do you mean?" He told me not to take the pickup! "Real funny, Shane" "Well," he said, "it still has an ignition and a steering wheel. Don't take the pickup!"

You know he could be a prankster too. One time he got anelastic and put it around the sprayer hose on the kitchen sink and faced it at the front so when I turned on the sink, I would get sprayed! Wrong. Our daughter-in-law came over to visit. She came in the door, greeting us, and turned to the sink. Got a glass and turned on the faucet! Of course she got it right in the face! Shane was bent over laughing. Me, I know now what he had been up to. I was saved from the harsh treatment. "These are the fun times." Shane loves apple pie. He said if there isn't apple pie, there is no pie. So at Thanksgiving time, we decide to have some fun with this. Everyone has been let in on the joke. All were supposed to say they want apple pie when asked. You know how the cook always says: who wants pumpkin, etc. I always make three pumpkin, one apple, a chocolate for Jenny. The look on his face when most everyone said they wanted apple!

Cooking

My cooking should be called "burnt offerings." I found a cookbook called that, so I had to have it. I decided to invite our girls and their families over for dinner. I had a couple of frozen chickens, and thought, *Well, if I put these chickens in the pressure cooker first, then I can take all the meat off them and make soup for supper.* The chicken cooked and the meat in a soup pan with chicken broth, onions, and carrots out of the garden. Everything was ready, but to put in the noodles. Timing's good, the girls would be here any time now, so I got out the package of store-bought noodles and began to add to this beautiful pot of soup. I started to add the noodles, and it's the end of the package, so I decide to just finish it off and dump in the rest. Oh my hell, what's that floating on the top of the soup! Weevils, weevils, I totally freaked out! They must have been in the noodles. By now everyone was there, looking at the soup! Now what was I going to do? Just about in tears, I grabbed the pot and headed downstairs and dumped it. So much for dinner! Our daughter, Angie, saved the occasion by going home and bringing over some tinfoil-wrapped dinners she had prepared. Bless her heart. I guess that cleaning out all the old stuff from the cabinets would be my next project. And I would be making homemade noodles from now on!

Some girlfriends and I used to belong to a bowling team. We used to go every Tuesday morning. One day after we were finished, the girls wanted to go to lunch. I declined, as I told them that I was going home to make bread, hamburger soup, and pumpkin pies. We had a kitchen in the basement for bread making, and there I got the bread going. Upstairs to do the soup I went. When I finished chopping all the vegetables and the soup was cooking, I then went to the root cellar for the home-canned pumpkin. Put some bread in oven while I was downstairs and then started the pies. Shane came home, and I served soup and hot bread. When I finished eating dinner, I jumped up to get the pie, as I had been craving the pie all day. Serve myself a nice portion, with whipping cream. The first bite, yuck!" I spit it out and said to Shane, "What the heck, what is this taste!" All of a sudden, I knew and asked him if when he canned the pumpkin, he labeled it. He said, "Did you use my apricot nectar? Well, have you ever tasted apricot in pumpkin?" I walked straight to the trash and dumped the three pies in it. I should have gone to lunch with the girls!

You know when cooking, it pays to look and see what the label says. One time I was again making bread. I was mixing it all up and now just adding enough flour to finish. The dough was sticky, and the more flour I put in, the stickier it seemed to get! I went ahead and made loaves. This was not an easy process as it was so darned sticky, I couldn't figure this out. This had never happened before, and I have made bread for years. After I had the loaves in the oven and was putting away things, I came upon the 10-pound flour sack. I now noticed it says "Pancake Flour!" Duh! Talk about heavy bread!

When my girlfriend Terry and I got to know each other, we invited her and her husband Jim to dinner one evening. We were all set at the table, and she asked me if I have any napkins (as her Jim had a beard and was always getting food in it). I knew that I didn't but got up to find something. I didn't have any paper towels, napkins, nothing that I could think of. Then I grabbed some coffee filters and passed them around, saying this was the next best thing. Terry laughed and said she had never had anyone hand her a coffer filters for a napkin! I received homemade napkins from her for Christmas the following year. I also had made me some and never to be without it again!

Have you ever made your own salad dressing for green salad? Again, read the label! I made a salad for dinner one night and mixed up the dressing for it. We had dinner, and I was doing the dishes when I picked up the gallon vinegar jar to put it away and noticed that it said "Fish Fertilizer!" (I kept a jar under the sink with the vinegar, as I didn't have a lot of storage space.) I was laughing so hard and said to Shane, "Boy, am I glad I didn't have any salad tonight." He asked me why. To this day, he wants to know what's in the salad dressing.

Our friend Lee told me about the best steak he had ever eaten, it was at a restaurant, and he was watching them cook it. He said that they poured salt all over the grill and slapped the steaks on. Yep, the best he has ever had. So I decide to try this. Don't ever!

I was working at my hair salon in town, and our son Scott called and asked if he could cook some chili for dinner. Great by me. (I hate cooking, can you tell?) I told him to get our big kettle out and cover the beans with a lot of water then boil until done. He called me a couple hours later and said, "Mom, the beans are all the way to the top of the kettle!" I can't tell you how many pounds of beans there were. When I got home, we had to find another pan and remove half the beans. It worked out fine, but we gave him a time about it.

Speaking of things not to do.

Never wash your baby potatoes in the washing machine! I always sorted out the babies from the medium and the large, as I liked to can these little ones. I would put them in the washer and then let it agitate for about a minute. Then would take them out, rinse the washer out, and then wash the potatoes off under hot water before putting into the jars. They would come out so nice. A couple of years of this, and one day I could smell something bad while the dryer was going. The clothes smelled pretty bad too! I kept complaining to Shane about the odor. He proceeded to pull the back off the dryer to see what might be wrong. Nothing there, so he started checking the washer. In between the drum and the tub was a muck of mud! Potato washing, I presumed. Then he was cleaning all that out, and the screwdriver he was using slipped and punched a hole in the drum. Now we needed a new washer. You can guess I wasn't real popular!

Never ever pour leftover spaghetti sauce out in the toilet! I tried this. When the toilet plugs up and overflows, and really overflows, you might have a couple of hours of cleaning up to do. (I mean real red and real greasy!) And it doesn't come easy! Never use hairspray for deodorant! (Cold and sticky.) Never use Arthritis Hot for toothpaste! (I wondered why my mouth was burning!) Never back up riding lawn mower into electric fence! Then don't step off while the fence is shocking you, it just gets worse! Never go swimming in a pool (especially one with chlorine in it) after having an ingrown toenail taken off! Never laugh at your husband while he is yelling at you. My darling husband went to milk Suzie Cow one day. All of a sudden, I heard him yelling at me. "What's the matter, Shane?" I could see him down at the barn but couldn't see what's wrong. I got closer, and there he stood with hay and straw all over him—the chain saw running, the cow kicking up and tearing around. I looked at the cow station and it's torn apart, and I knew what happened. He had decided (after he locked the cow's head in) to take the chain saw, and make more room between the boards, not thinking of the fact that she might not appreciate this. Well, you know she backed out of the thing, pulling boards and all with her! Ran over Shane on her way out! Now he was waving his hands, hollering at me to go back in the house, as YOU think everything's. funny! IT WAS.

Our Sense of Humor

Sometimes Shane can't take a joke. We had gone to bed one cold winter evening, it was twenty below outside, and we lived in a trailer at this time, and they weren't insulated very well. I was freezing and kept turning my side of the electric blanket up, and Shane was turning his side down, complaining that it's hot. Fifteen minutes of this, and he jumped out of bed and turned on the light, grabbed the blanket and looked at it. "You put the blanket on upside down"! He yelled at me. (Putting his controls on my side, and my controls on his side.) No wonder he was sweating, I mean, beads of sweat covered his forehead, and I was shaking! I was so cold!

Another dayoour son Mike was out with his dad and brothers working. Dad was sawing, and the boys were stacking the logs. I went out there. Just about that time, I saw Mike throwing the cut logs at an angle behind him in a pile. "Hey, Mike, you might want to be careful, you might hit your dad." (Shane was sawing and couldn't hear this.) Mike couldn't either, I guess, because the next throw got Shane right in the head! Thank God he dropped the chain saw as he went down. He wasn't out for very long, but the look on Mike's face was priceless!

This story can seem to be so silly, but strange things happen. The day that Shane and our boys were putting the roof on our barn, I had been getting ready to fix lunch, and I got a phone call and had to go to town. I had a pot of beans on cooking and thought I'd ask Mike if he wanted to come in and fix some corn bread. He said yes, and I left for town. I wasn't gone very long, and when we all got ready to eat lunch, I sat the cake pan down on the table, telling everyone how nice of a job Mike had done with the corn bread. While I was saying this, I was cutting pieces for everyone. I took the first bite. What the hell? As I was spitting the stuff out in to the trash can. "How much salt did you put in this?" Mike said, "One cup." I looked at him, and he pointed at his dad and said, "He said so." Mike had gone out and hollered up at his dad at the barn. "How much salt, Dad?" Well, we know that he doesn't always hear all that is said. Not paying much attention to the question, he said one cup. Shane deigned this, of course. Anyway, we said that we would just feed the corn bread to the chickens. Wrong, the next day the chickens were dying with their necks stretched out, and the rest were dead! Too much salt, maybe. Never feed corn bread to the chickens! (Heavy-salted corn bread anyways.)

One day when our daughter was about fourteen, her dad was outside working on something, and she was trying to get his attention. She's saying, "Dad." No answer, again "Dad." No answer. "Dad!" He hadn't answered yet, so she yelled "Dad" real loud. He yelled back, "WHAT?" Well, she came in just laughing, and he came in mad and shaking his head, saying, "You can't get any peace around here." As we girls were all laughing. He sat down, and our other daughter, Angie, went over to him and proceeded to rub silly putty on his head and then rubbed it in. All this before he even knew what was gong on. Never push your luck!

Bear in Yard

One sunny day, Shane and I were working out in the yard, and we went around back where our picnic table was. We sat down and were enjoying a cup of coffee. Shane told me he really didn't feel very well. I said, "Why don't you just lie down in the lounge chair for a while then." This he did. I decided to go around front again and work on whatever we had been doing. I got around there and remembered that I had forgotten my cup. So I went back around, and there I could see Shane was asleep already. I was thinking to myself that he must not feel good to go to sleep that fast. And just about that time, I reached over to the table to pick up the cup, and out of the top of my vision, I noticed a movement across the table from me. I looked up and there stood a bear. The bear was swinging his head around and over the table (evidently looking for something to eat!). I didn't quite know what to do, I then said very quietly to Shane, "Wake up, there's a bear." The bear looked up just then, kinda moved his head over the table, looked at me, then turned and ran off. Thank you God. Coffee with the bears, anyone?

Just Funnies

My sister-in-law Sherry was at our house with the kids. We had just had chocolate cake, and there on the floor was some of the chocolate frosting. I bent over and picked up the frosting, squeezing it between my thumb and forefinger to get it. Then I decided to smell it! Don't ask me why, I just did. It wasn't chocolate at all! It was the stuff out of one of the kid's diapers!

In Northern Idaho, we have what we call stink bugs. They smell very bad when they let go of the stuff. Well, I was sleeping and something in the corner of my eye was tickling me. I reached up to touch my eye, and something was burning it. Now I smelled the stink. It was a stinkbug right in the corner of my eye giving it to me! What a way to wake up.

Our Jenny had a broken ankle. One evening, she decided to go in and take a shower. A few minutes later, I was walking by the bathroom, and I heard a quiet "Oh my." I thought about that for a minute, and I couldn't remember any of the kids ever saying, "Oh my." So I opened the bathroom door to see. There on the floor sat Jenny, two legs straightened out in front of her and one leg with a bag on it—the other leg with the cast on it (as not to get the cast wet). I said, "What was the 'Oh my' for?" She said, "I bagged the wrong leg." Good one, Jen.

Have you heard of the saying "Don't cry over split milk"? One morning, Shane brought in the fresh milk from the cow. This bucket holds four gallons. I took it to put on the counter and accidentally caught the counter as it is going up. You can't guess the places all that milk went. Jenny patted me on the shoulder telling me, "Not to cry, Mom, you'll get it cleaned up."

I'll never forget the dirty look this certain lady was giving me while at the laundry mat. My small son Pete and I were there doing the laundry. He was sitting at one end of the long tables. (They had these tables there to fold clothes on.) He had crawled down there and was just sitting there playing quietly. As I was folding clothes, he started to cry. I looked up and couldn't see anything wrong, so I asked him, "What's the matter, sweetie?" I noticed this lady giving me this look. Well, I went down to my boy to see, and there pinned on his lip was a clothespin! Guess that's why I was getting the dirty look!

Our youngest daughter, Angie, was quite the little character. When she was little, (about eighteen months) whenever her dad was fixing something around the house, he would reach to get a tool that had just been there, and it would be gone. She seemed to delight in taking them and hiding them, then showing her dad where she had hid them.

The girls and I were taking a trip. The weather was hot. I kept a spray bottle in the car so the girls could spray me with it. To keep me awake or cool me off, whatever, we were going through this construction line. We could only go about seven miles an hour. Angie had the spray bottle, and there's this worker standing along the side. She decided that this fellow looked too hot, so she squirted him. He didn't know what happened! I mean, he jumped a mile. Didn't have a clue, poor guy.

Some Dog Stories

One night, my girls decided they wanted mom to sleep out on the lawn with them. Well, this wasn't my favorite thing to do, but I said OK, just this once. We had fun telling stories, and after fighting to get comfortable, I went to sleep, only to be awakened by this atrocious smell! It was just getting dawn, and I opened my eyes, trying to find out what that smell was. There lying right in front of my face was our English sheepdog, Ruben. He was letting the biggest farts, right in my face! That's it; I went inside, no more gatherings on the lawn.

Tending my friend Terry's dog was a night to remember too. I had a greyhound dog from the racetracks. He was a good dog. Terry had a Great Dane dog named Midnight, he was big and black. When time came to go to bed this one evening, my dog usually laid by our bed. Well, Midnight wanted to do the same. He would try to come in the room by peeking in the door (which was not totally closed). Each time he tried to peek in, my dog Jamer would growl at him. I finally told Shane that if I wanted any sleep, I was going to have to sleep on the sofa. I went in the living room, lay down, and here came Midnight. He put his head right up on my shoulder, and there we were together. I tried to sleep for a while but couldn't with this dog on my shoulder. "Midnight, you are to put your head on the floor." Cute, huh? Anyway, the next day, my dad and mom came to visit. I was still tending the dog. We were in the kitchen, and Midnight was lying there looking at us. His front legs were straight out, and I noticed his long toenails. So I decided to paint them. Red would work. He lay there, very still while I painted them. Dad and mom were real impressed, I'm sure. Terry's husband Jim said that when he left the dog, he was male, and when he came to get him, he turned female—red nails and all!

Going the Wrong Way

Have you ever sent the wrong presents to the wrong people? I was asking my dad about the gift I had sent them for Christmas. He then told me that I sent our son Mike's present to them and that means that I must have sent dad and moms present to Mike. So then they both had to forward to each another!

What's embarrassing about this? Our friends, Sam and Maxine and Cecil and Myrt and Shane and I, all went to dinner one evening to celebrate Cecil and Myrt's anniversary. Myrt opened the card from us, she looked up at me and said, "Sam and Maxine?" I put the wrong name on the card of course!

Rhonda and I:
Taylorsville

You know, two friends living together can be quite fun: being twenty-one, on your own, sharing responsibilities, and loving each and every precious moment. We had bought a car. Must have cost all of $25.00. There was a window missing, no muffler; we didn't have money for plates, and we liked to go dancing at the local pub. After going out one evening, a group of us all went to the Roadway Inn afterward for coffee and breakfast. We were all sitting at a round table. It seemed there was a break in the conversation, and as I was sipping my coffee, a drip (from my nose) dropped in my cup! Total silence. I didn't even want to look up! Plus the trip home in the car was really scary; because of all the chances we were taking. Will the police get us for no muffler, then no plates? If none of that happens, maybe we won't freeze to death before we get home! Well, we lived through it, only to be scared out of our wits the next day. We were fixing breakfast, and we heard a sound coming from the storage shed. This shed is actually part of the house, but the entrance door is on the outside. The door opened to the inside of shed. One morning, as we were fixing pancakes for our kids, we heard some strange sounds; they seem to be coming from the shed. We talked about the sound. "What the heck is in the shed? Maybe one of the neighbor kids?" There it went again. Who is going to go look? OK, I will. When I got out there, the door was ajar about two inches. I slightly pushed the door, asking, "Who's in here?" The door slammed shut! I got down on my knees to look under it, and I could see some sort of wood along the bottom of the door. I tried to open it again and no way, this door was totally not moving. "Hey, Rhonda, come on out here and help me get in the shed." She was not going to do this. She said that she heard about a big guy escaping from the state pen, and you never know who or what could be going on in there. So OK, we didn't do anything. I guess we just forgot because later that day, I had a date to go play cards at some friend's house. About halfway through the game, the phone rang and it's Rhonda. I took the call, and she's all yelling at me for leaving her home alone with the thing in the shed! She said she called the cops because the strange sounds kept happening. "OK, I'll be right there." When I got there, the policeman had, with flashlight in one hand and pistol in the other, kicked the door in! From up high, coming straight at him was a set of eyes! He shot about the time the big cat (as in cougar) was flying by his head! The cat must have gone in there in the night, and when I was pushing on the door, he moved and must have jumped up to a shelf, knocking over a set of twin bunk bed's frames! This was what lodged in front of the door. Who only knows what would have happened to me had I got inside with the cat! Rhonda gave me a hard time about leaving her with the critter. Some friend, huh?

In the fall, (same place) along came the earwigs. I was coming inside from hanging out clothes, and there on the door were hundreds of earwigs. I had an idea, I grabbed a dishcloth and swooped up a bunch of the wigs, then went inside to scare my friend. I found the bathroom door closed, so I asked if I could come in. I opened the door, and there she was sitting on the throne. "Perfect!" I shook the dishcloth over the top of her (earwigs falling all over her), and she fell off the toilet trying to get away, screaming not-so-nice obscenities at me. Can you imagine! I couldn't stop laughing forever. We still talked about the things we did to each another.

We remember the good times. Being poor and not having a washer prompted this episode. We girls were out sun tanning in the yard one sunny afternoon (bikinis in those days). Out of the corner of my eye, I saw a pickup truck coming along. It stopped at the stop sign by us. I jumped up, running over to the corner, and hollered at the fellow. "Are you going to the dump with that Dexter double-load washer?" He said, "I sure am, missy." Then asked me if I wanted the machine. "Please." He backed up, and we unloaded it. He took it up and into the house for me. The girls were so . . . embarrassed. They couldn't believe that I would do that. "Hey, when you need something, you can't be too proud!"

Don't Let the "Small Stuff" Scare You

I had moved into an apartment of my own, and one night, a friend named Sandy called to see if I wanted to go out dancing. (She would pick me up, and afterwards drop me off.) I went into the house about 3:00 a.m. and winged the door shut. It stayed open about six inches. My living room door had a window, and curtains hung there also. They were open, maybe six to eight inches. I had just taken off my blouse and glanced at the door. There was a guy's face plastered to the window, looking in, and the door was not completely shut! I immediately got mad. Straight to the door and slammed it shut. The guy jumped back and took off, running around the duplex. (I could hear his steps, he was running so hard.) About that time, I realize what I just did. My heart's pounding, and I ran and locked all doors. I didn't have a phone and vehicle at that time! I sat up all night looking at the curtains for a shadow to pass. The streetlights from outside and the apartment dark, you could see if anyone went by. I really didn't know what I would of done if he had come back!

Driving

I remember my dad teaching me to drive. We had a push-button car. Yes, you pushed the buttons instead of using a stick shift. We were going up this hill to our home; the hill was about a six-percent grade. Pop was telling me that when you are climbing and pulling a hill, you could push the number 2 button. OK, so I did this and then he said to push the drive button. OK, that's easy. Then I pushed the number 2 button again. He said to push the drive, I did, and then the number 2 again. I was thinking that because of this hill, that's what he wanted. Wrong. He sort of gave up, said something about he couldn't teach me to drive.

Not too many years later, I was at the Dairy Queen. I bought a black raspberry marshmallow malt. It was a large, and in one of those tall paper cup things. I started down the road, not thinking about anything except getting home. I lifted my malt to mouth (no lid or straw) take a drink, and the next thing I knew, the malt was coming down the front of me in full force! Moral of the story is to place malt cup on the bottom set of lips instead of the top before dumping.

I don't know about you but one of my rules of thumb has always been to get dressed properly before going somewhere, right? OK, so one morning, I had to get the children off to school, and I decided to just go (still in my huge thick bathrobe), thinking that everything would be all right and hoping that no one sees me. I dropped off the kids. I started to proceed down the road toward home, and the car won't shift out of first gear! I decided to cross the street and ask my neighbor if he would check it out for me. I was knocking on their door at eight in the morning in this bathrobe. After the funny looks and the story, he said, "Sure, he will take it for a drive. Just go in and have coffee and wait." Awhile later, the door opened and there stood Don as white as a ghost! "What the heck is wrong? Don, you don't look to good." He told us that he's driving up the highway, testing the car and going about sixty when the hood on my big Tornado car came flying open! Scared the BG's out of him. Yes, he got to a stop and thankfully wasn't killed. The transmission shifted just fine!

Then another time, I went to one of those sidewalk sales the stores have. I was smoking a cigarette, finished and threw it out the window (back in those days when this wasn't a no-no). I was thinking about the kind of things I wanted to get for our family. I got pillows, clothes, enough stuff that a store helper had to help pack it out. When we got to my car, we saw that there's a fire in the backseat! A little ole couple was standing there watching as the store helper threw down the stuff and opened the door and proceeded to pull the backseat out. He runs it over to a drinking fountain, holds the seat over it putting out the fire! I was standing there in shock, knowing very well how the fire got started! The helper brought the seat back and told us that someone must have thrown a cigarette in the window by mistake. I heard the couple saying, "Can you believe anyone would do that to the little gal's car?" My seat was ruined, the car didn't smell too good and I couldn't decide whether to cop up to my better half or leave the story with the couple!

One day, I had an appointment in Spokane. I took our Isuzu Trooper. I was going along on the freeway, and all of a sudden, it sounded like someone had shot my rig! And the popping sounds just kept coming. I pulled over and got out to check the car. I was seeing a total flat tire, with no tread left. So I went around to the back and bent down, looking at the instructions for using the jack (which I didn't even know where it was yet). Then I heard a rig coming to a screeching halt right behind me. It sounded like it was going to hit me before it could stop. I hurried and turned around to look, and there was a pickup. Two teenage boys, both hanging out the window, asked if I need any help. What I saw was steam just flowing up and out of their radiator and engine area. (The boys hadn't seemed to notice.) I walked toward them and said, "Yes, and so do you!" Then the driver noticed the steam and jumped out, and they lifted the hood. They had a hole in the radiator. I told them that I would make them a deal. If they would change the tire for me, I would take them to a phone for help. We all got to our destinations.

I hope this hasn't happened to you. I was going to town one day and I backed out off the driveway, Jenny and Clint were sitting on the porch. When I came home, there laid our dog in the driveway. Dead. The kids were crying and asking me how come I didn't stop when I ran over him. I said that I thought it was a ball. How do you explain something like that?

Have you ever scared the heck out of a police officer? I have, and it was so fun. Pete and I were going to the bank. We used the drive-up window, and as we are pulling up, I had let the engine compression build up. And as we pulled in, so did an officer next to us, to use the services himself. Just as we both got there, my rig backfired, and we jumped a mile and looked over at the officer. He was looking all around and nervous looking, and we realized what happened and just broke out laughing. Then looking over, he said, "What the heck?" We told him our rig just backfired! He thought he'd been shot at or something of the sort!

Some Good Luck

Shane and I had been talking about selling a horse for the money to buy a calf. We planned on raising a calf to butcher in the fall. As luck has it, this one day I was going to the doctor's and listening to the Swap Shop on the radio. The ad being given was for someone to trade a quarter buffalo, three quarter beef, for maybe a horse? I pulled over and called the number on my cell phone. I asked the lady not to trade until I can talk to my husband and call her back that evening. Shane said no way, as he had plans to breed the horse for a mule! The next day, we were headed ninety miles to the farm and traded for the one-fourth buffalo beef. Worked out great. We didn't have to sell the horse and didn't have to buy the calf. I loved it.

Here I am helping Shane. He asked me to hold these two iron gates while he did some work on them. The next thing I knew, they had dropped on all ten of my toes! I couldn't put shoes on for three weeks or so. They might not have been broken, but they sure felt like it!

When we were building our log house, we had plywood up for doors (temporarily). You stepped up on this log to go in and just push on the door. But if you were going out, you needed to pull on this sixteen-penny nail to close it behind you. I had told Shane that the nail was exactly at my eye level. Well, you know how it goes. The nail did not get removed soon enough, because I went to step up and in, and there was a small rug on the other side of the door. And as I went to push the door in, it caught on the rug, and my eye and the nail collided! The nail went into and around my eye, coming out the other side of my eye! I remember holding my hand over it, screaming, and Shane trying to get me to move the hand so he could see it. He said he was taking me to the hospital, and I said no. So he called the doctor, and he wanted me to go in. OK, we went. My eye was completely bloodshot and swollen shut, but was still there. I knew the doctor thought that Shane had hit me! Luckily I still have my eye. The nail disappeared.

Rotten Egg

When my son Scott and I were going to work one day, we got in the car and took off. He said that he could smell something that smelled like rotten eggs. I took a smell and couldn't smell rotten eggs. He said that he could. A few days later, it was evening, and we were playing cards with out friends, Myrt and Cecil. Our daughter Angie asked me if she could clean out my purse. I told her to go ahead, just not to lose anything. A few minutes later, she came over with this thing in her hand and said, "What's this, Mom?" The thing was all cracked, discolored, ugly and stank just like a rotten egg! My son, Scott, started in, "I told you I smelled rotten egg!" Oh my hell, that was exactly what it was. I had the habit of taking boiled eggs to work so I would have something easy to eat when I needed to. Guess I missed that one! What was wrong with my smeller? The worst of it was, who had I stood by in the stores, etc., who could also smell rotten eggs?

The last of my antics: My husband needed a haircut, so I sat up to do the job for him. I trimmed all around the line I wanted, looked to see if the sideburns were even, and said, "Yep, there you go, hon." (As I was taking off the apron.) We took off to visit some friends. While driving down the road, I looked over at him and realized that I just trimmed the hairline and didn't cut his hair!

This book could go on forever, but will not. My family says it's a never-ending saga! I hope you had a few good laughs as I did while remembering and writing these stories.

All the names in this book are real except mine. I have to protect the innocent!

Oh, just one more: I remember the day we
butchered fifty chickens. The next day I went
to the grocery store to do our two-week shopping.
While I was unpacking the groceries, Shane
looks in a bag and he wanted to know "Are these chickens
better than the ones we put in the freezer yesterday"?

"AS ALWAYS, ONLY YOU GIRL."

Made in the USA
Las Vegas, NV
02 February 2022

42898126R00057